La Salle and the Rise of New France

*Dedicated to all the Goddesses and Angels
who have helped make this series possible*

Janet Snider and Betty Sherwood

canchron books
Canadian Chronicles

Toronto, Canada

Acknowledgements

We wish to thank the following people for their support and assistance during the creation of this book: Scott Bradford, Jim Casquenette, Jacqueline Snider, Jean Shippey, Paula Letheren, Rachelle Mack, Ruth Sherwood, George Goodwin, Anne Marie Fryer, Leslie B. Koster, Aron Slipacoff, Maggie Blondeau, Deborah Cooper, Sara Kligman, Marilyn Dodds, Laura Cairns, Judith Walker, Adam Kosior (pilot), Mary Wolfe, Staff of the Toronto Public Library, Staff of Library and Archives Canada

Original Cover Map Design Copyright © 2005 Paula Letheren
Copyright © 2005 canchron books
Text and Design Copyright © 2005 canchron books
Design Rachelle Mack

Canadian Heritage   Patrimoine canadien

This project has been supported by the Canadian Studies Program, Department of Canadian Heritage; the opinions expressed do not necessarily reflect the views of the Government of Canada.

Library and Archives Canada Cataloguing in Publication

Snider, Janet, 1944-
La Salle and the Rise of New France /
Janet Snider and Betty Sherwood.

(Explorer chronicles)
Includes bibliographical references and index.
ISBN 0-9688049-3-4

1. La Salle, Robert Cavelier de, 1643-1687--Juvenile literature.
2. Canada--History--To 1763 (New France)--Juvenile literature.
3. Explorers--North America--Biography--Juvenile literature.
4. Explorers--France--Biography--Juvenile literature.
I. Sherwood, Betty, 1943- II. Title. III. Series.

FC362.1.L37S65 2005 j971.01'63'092   C2005-903919-1
Print Production by Tibbles Bird & Company, Toronto, Canada

Contents

New France

The first European settlements in Canada were established by the Vikings in Newfoundland around 1000 AD. Jacques Cartier, a French explorer, stayed in present day Québec City in 1535.

Pont-Gravé set up a trading post at Tadoussac which was visited by Champlain in 1603. It was in 1604 that Champlain settled on the St. Croix River in New Brunswick and in 1605 at Port Royal in Nova Scotia. Acadia had begun. The Canadian shores had been familiar to European fisherman for centuries, but Champlain was the first to establish a settlement at Québec in 1608.

Keeping the settlement alive was difficult because few French citizens wanted to emigrate. King Louis XIII was not very supportive of the colony. It was not a great source of riches. Champlain asked priests to come to New France to provide leadership to the settlers and to convert the Native people to Christianity. Several Recollet priests arrived in 1615. The Jesuits took up the challenge in 1625 because they considered missionary work a duty. Their annual reports, the "Jesuit Relations", were read avidly by the French people.

Ville-Marie in 1642 after W. Décary (1886)

Paul de Chomedey de Maisonneuve, the Founder of Montréal. Places d'Armes, Montréal

that bordered Iroquois territory. It was not successful as a mission but became Montréal, a commercial centre for the fur trade in the 1650's. Between 1642 and 1667, it was raided by the Iroquois, which made fur trading and farming hazardous. In spite of the dangers, merchants, skilled workers, soldiers and professional men came with their wives and children. Some of the surnames, familiar to the present day were: Boucher, Giroux, Bélanger, Morin, Mercier, Auber, Amyot, Drouin, Coté, Tardif, Cloutier and Hébert.

When Champlain died in 1635, the population of New France was less than 300. Most lived in Québec City, with some in Trois-Rivières, Tadoussac and Acadia. In 1642 Ville-Marie was established by a religious group of people who built a missionary city. The leader was Paul de Chomedey de Maisonneuve. He and Jeanne Mance, a devout woman, and a small group of people built an outpost in the wilderness

Louis Hébert, Apothecary

Jeanne Mance, 1606-1673

A settlement was built at Trois-Rivières where there was fertile land, good fishing and beaches for landing canoes.

Between 1642 and 1652, there were only 10 marriages performed in New France with 22 births and 23 deaths. Iroquois raids were common, so very few French wanted to live in New France. All this changed in 1665 when King Louis XIV took an interest in the colony and sent the Carignan Regiment of soldiers to defend against the Iroquois.

The soldiers built forts along the Richelieu River. When the Iroquois saw this show of strength, they requested a treaty. Peace had finally come to the small colony. The King appointed Jean Talon as the first Intendant of New France. Talon described New France to his superiors in France as having healthful climate, immense forests, fertile soil, abundant furs and possible mineral wealth. He envisioned a much larger colony with unlimited potential.

King Louis took a particular interest in the colony. He sent the "King's daughters", girls who had been orphaned and were of child-bearing age, to New France to be married. There might be 30 weddings at one time. When the Carignan Regiment was demobilized in New France, soldiers were offered land and wives.

1605
Spanish writer Miguel de Cervantes completed "Don Quixote".

1605
Willem Janszoon made the first European sighting of Australia.

1609-1610
Henry Hudson explored Hudson Strait and Bay.

The People of New France

New France was reserved for Catholic settlers. In 1665 400 members of the Carignan Regiment stayed in New France, married and became landowners. Labourers, known as engagés, came for three-year contracts; half of them stayed. Seven hundred and seventy-five "King's daughters" arrived between 1663 and 1673. 90% of them got married. Mother Marie de l'Incarnation founded the Ursuline Convent in Québec City. The nuns looked after the women when they arrived. Mother Marie made sure that the women understood that settled men with farms would be the best husbands.

The colonists lived longer than people did in France and babies had a higher survival rate. A couple had to clear a half-hectare (1.25 acres) of land each year. That required a lot of hard work. Clearing and building occupied a farmer and his wife for their whole lives, so large families were a blessing. Also, grants were given to fathers with big families, so having 10 to 15 children was common. Louis Dechene, historian, described the life of a habitant farmer, "At his death, 30 years after he received the concession (land), he possesses 30 arpents of arable land, a bit of meadow, a barn, a stable, a slightly more spacious house, neighbours and a pew in the church. His life has passed clearing and building." Clearing the land was as important to the colony as winning battles with the Natives. The land made possible a permanent settlement along the St. Lawrence River.

Habitants grew wheat, corn, barley, oats, tobacco, vegetables, and animals that produced meat, milk and eggs. They were well fed compared to the poor living in cities in France. They made tools, woollen and linen fabrics and used hand-cured leather to make shoes.

The "coureurs de bois" were men who travelled westward to trade furs directly with Native trappers. At first coureurs de bois were unlicensed because the merchants wanted the fur trading centre to be in Montréal. In 1681 the coureurs de bois became legitimate and were called "voyageurs". The explorers could not have travelled so far to advance the fur trade and open North America without the voyageurs' strength and knowledge of the wilderness.

The King decreed that the suitable marriage ages were 18 for men and 14 for women. Bachelors who did not marry within 14 days, when brides were available, lost their hunting, fishing and fur trading rights. Talon set up permanent communities for the Huron and Algonquin near the French towns. The King offered a wedding present of 150 livres to Native women who married Frenchmen.

1610
The first shipment of tea to Europe was made by Dutch traders.

1610
Thomas Harriott discovered sunspots.

1611
Marco de Dominus published his scientific explanation of a rainbow.

Mother Marie de l'Incarnation said, "A Frenchman goes Native more easily than an Indian becomes French." The plan was not very successful. Native women felt too restricted in French houses and society and sometimes were known to slip out the window and disappear. The colony did expand and become prosperous. Talon made the following additions: horses, sheep, pigs, a tannery, brewery, hat making, lumbering to supply masts for the ships of LaRochelle, tar manufacturing, a shipyard, a lead mine in Gaspé, an iron mine at Trois-Rivières and a coal mine in Québec. By 1672, during Talon's second term of office, there were 700 births per year. In 1681 the population was 10,000. It was Talon's vision of expansion and economic progress that set the stage and made LaSalle's explorations possible.

The First Shipyard in Canada by Rex Woods, 1956

Jean Talon established the first shipyard in Canada in 1670. Even though some of Talon's ventures were not successful, historian Gustave Lânctot wrote, "With scanty means at his disposal, he had accomplished the magnificent task of peopling an empty colony and infusing it with economic life."

René-Robert Cavelier, Sieur de La Salle
(1643-1687)

Cavelier de LaSalle 300th Anniversary

LaSalle was born in Rouen on November 21, 1643. His father, Jean, was a wealthy merchant and landowner. One of his estates was called LaSalle, which he gave to René-Robert. This is how LaSalle got his name. LaSalle's father wanted him to have a good education and he could afford the best. The Jesuits, the Society of Jesus, had a reputation for being superior educators, so at first, LaSalle went to a local Jesuit grammar school. At 15 he went to Paris and joined the Jesuits in preparation for the priesthood. He was extremely good at mathematics, but he also studied Greek, Latin, Hebrew, Arabic, Spanish and Italian. No doubt his ability with languages helped him to master the Native languages when he was travelling in North America.

The Jesuits were missionaries, so they travelled a great deal. They knew the value of educating their pupils in the areas of study that would help them as priests and missionaries. Their courses included logic, astronomy, geography and navigation. LaSalle attended Collège Henri IV where he was taught to sight with an astrolabe and he learned the principles of map-making. When he graduated he was sent to teach grammar at three different boys' schools.

He didn't like the work, so he requested he be sent to the Jesuit mission in China. The Jesuits disapproved of his bold initiative. He had withstood the disciplined life at school: getting up at 5 a.m., going to bed at 9 p.m., with study hall, lectures, prayers and classroom presentations in between. He was too independent and stubborn to be told what to do when he was over twenty. When he requested a teaching position in Portugal and was again turned down, he resigned from the Jesuit order. The Father Superior realized that LaSalle was too ambitious and hotheaded to be a successful priest. LaSalle was admired for his intelligence and his good moral behaviour so he was able to leave the priesthood without scandal.

LaSalle left France in 1667 and travelled to Montréal, the most dangerous settlement in New France at the time. His older brother, Jean, was a Sulpician priest there. The Order of St. Sulpice owned land on the frontier and was giving out tracts of land to settlers. There was a real possibility of becoming rich from trading and owning land in this new country. LaSalle had given up his inheritance rights when he had entered the Jesuit order, but his brothers and sisters gave him a yearly allowance of 400 livres when he went to New France.

Estate at La Chine

Montréal was near the Iroquois warpaths, so was often raided. In spite of the danger, LaSalle took several thousand acres of land west of the town and named the estate St. Sulpice.

1619
Jens Munk, a Dane, made the first European visit to the Churchill River.

1620
English Pilgrims landed at Plymouth Bay.

1620
The contrabassoon (double bassoon) was invented.

He kept 400 acres for his personal use and then offered 50 acre lots to settlers. They cleared 25 acres of forest each year. The rocks removed from the fields were used to build boundary fences and small buildings. LaSalle's estate was an outpost that stood guard against Iroquois raids on the town of Montréal.

Trading Post by the Lachine Canal in Montréal

A band of Seneca Iroquois spent the winter on LaSalle's estate. They talked about a river called the Ohio which flowed to the ocean. LaSalle believed that the river flowed to the Gulf of California and that this river was the western passage to China. He saw the possibility of trade and discovery. He was so determined to get to China that Montréalers called his estate, Lachine (China, in French).

LaSalle needed money to finance his expedition, so he began to trade furs for brandy. Trade and travel into the country required a permit, so LaSalle went to Québec City to speak to Governor Courcelles and the Provincial Administrator, Jean Talon. LaSalle's enthusiasm and detailed preparation impressed both of them. He was given permission in letters patent.

1625-1712
French astronomer Giovanni Cassini described the moons and rings of Saturn.

1637
Fifteen cm of snow fell on Huronia on May 19.

1638-1655
The colony of New Sweden on the Delaware River was soon taken over by the Dutch.

The governor and Talon wanted LaSalle to travel with two other explorers. One of the men, Dollier de Casson, had travelled a great deal in the forest. He was a huge man of 2 m in height (6 ft. 6 in.), who could lift 40 kg (100 lb.) above his head with one arm and knew the medicinal properties of many plants. The other man was Father Bréhan de Gallinée, a mapmaker.

Here they met more Seneca who invited them to their village. LaSalle, Gallinée and eight Frenchmen went along to the village. The others stayed to guard the canoes. They were welcomed and then overwhelmed with Seneca hospitality. Children brought them pumpkins and berries and they were invited to many feasts.

The First Expedition

The expedition left on July 6, 1669, with seven canoes and 24 men, including two medical practitioners, and the Seneca who had spent the winter with LaSalle acted as guides. They travelled 56 km (35 mi.) per day in still water. It took them 27 days to reach Lake Ontario. On August 11 they arrived at the present site of Rochester, New York.

Father Bréhan de Gallinée and Father François Dollier de Casson

Both men were Sulpician priests who were well educated and had many skills. Gallinée studied mathematics and astronomy and Dollier was an explorer, historian and architect.

Dollier said that he was one of three victims selected to go to Canada. He did adapt to life among the Native people and at one time decided that he would rather live with a welcoming tribe than return to Montréal. Dollier and Gallinée travelled with LaSalle at the governor's request. When they separated from LaSalle, the priests returned to Montréal by the northern route through Michilimackinac. It took them 347 days! Gallinée wrote an account of the journey and drew a map that was given to Talon. His journal was published in 1875. Dollier drew the plans for Notre-Dame Church, built in 1678. He also was involved in planning for the construction of the Lachine Canal.

LaSalle knew that he needed support and guides from the Seneca. They exchanged gifts of kettles, axes and knives for beaded necklaces. One day a group of warriors returned with a keg of brandy and proceeded to get drunk. LaSalle and Gallinée had been warned that alcohol could make Native people very violent and they knew they were in danger. They witnessed their first experience of torture when a young Native captive was tortured until he died. Europeans were cruel in the way they punished prisoners also, but that didn't make it easier to watch. After the frenzy had passed, LaSalle and Gallinée returned to Dollier and the others. They set out across Lake Ontario. Because it was late in the season, they did not go to see Niagara Falls but continued to Otinawatawa, [Hamilton, Ontario]. At this Iroquois village they found guides for the journey. One of the guides was a captive Shawnee, named Nika, who was given as a gift to LaSalle and stayed with him through all of his expeditions.

Marquette and Jolliet Sculpture in Chicago (detail)

In late August they met another Frenchman at a Native village. Louis Jolliet was returning from Lake Superior where Talon had sent him to search for copper mines. There were tribal wars among the Native people, so his explorations were too dangerous to continue. Jolliet was on his way back to New France. LaSalle and his party left to continue their explorations, but Dollier and Gallinée wanted to travel north to establish new missions.

Louis Jolliet (1645-1700)

Louis Jolliet was born in Beauport, near Québec City, and attended a Jesuit College in the late 1650's. He was talented musically and played the organ at church. When he was 25, Governor Talon sent Jolliet on an expedition to Lake Superior in search of copper mines. There was unrest among the Native tribes so his search was limited and unsuccessful. He spent the winter of 1670-71 in Sault Ste. Marie.

Frontenac arrived in New France in 1672. He commissioned Jolliet to find a route to the Sea of the South. Father Jacques Marquette, an interpreter, travelled with Jolliet. On the Mississippi, they went as far south as the Arkansas River. Natives in the area told them that the Mississippi River continued south to the Gulf of Mexico. Jolliet was a fine mapmaker, but he lost all his notes when his canoe capsized on the return journey to Montréal.

He mapped the Gulf of St. Lawrence and in appreciation for his important contribution he was given Anticosti Island. In 1697 he was made Royal Geographer of France. He died in 1700.

Over 300 years ago Jolliet suggested that building a 15 km canal would effectively connect Lake Michigan to the Gulf of Mexico. The Illinois and Michigan Canal was not built until 1848.

LaSalle was determined to find and follow the river that went southwest, so he pretended to be so ill that he could not travel. Dollier and Gallinée departed with a small party and left LaSalle to recover along with Nika and some coureurs de bois.

LaSalle continued south across Lake Erie towards the Ohio River. Their progress was slow because there were many fallen trees and ice was already forming on the water. The men were grumbling because of the hardships, but LaSalle was so determined that he hardly noticed their complaints. They got to the rapids at present-day Louisville, Kentucky, where the Ohio meets the Mississippi River and turns south. At this point the men were so fearful of continuing into unknown territory where they would get none of the glory or share in the riches, that they all disappeared. To desert in the wilderness and leave two men on their own was equal to murder.

1638
Jesuits watched an Iroquois game called "baggataway". They named it "jeu de la crosse".

1642
Dutch navigator Abel Tasman reached New Zealand.

1644
The Manchus proclaimed the Ch'ing Dynasty in China.

LaSalle and Nika turned back and arrived safely at LaChine, via the Ottawa River. The expedition had used up all of LaSalle's money, so he traded for furs on his return journey and arrived in Montréal with several canoes full of furs to sell. LaSalle was certain that he could find a practical route from the Great Lakes to the Mississippi River. This would enlarge the territory of New France to include the Midwest all the way to the Gulf of Mexico.

In 1671 he spoke to Talon about his desire to explore and trade in buffalo hides which make good leather for boots and saddles. Talon offered support but no money, so LaSalle went to the Sulpician Order that had provided his estate. The priests gave him enough money to buy trade goods for the Native people they would meet.

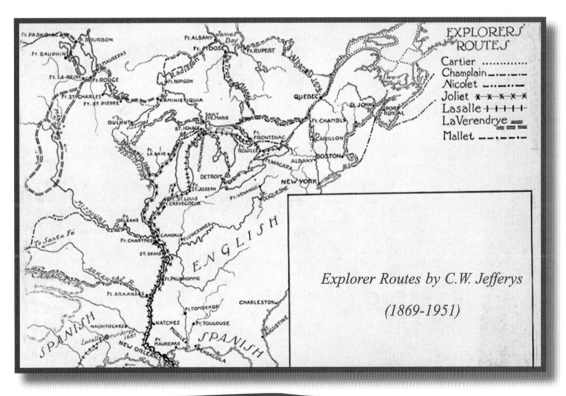

Explorer Routes by C.W. Jefferys

(1869-1951)

1644-1737
Antonio Stradivari, the Italian violinmaker, produced over 1,116 instruments.

1645
The word "backgammon" was coined for an ancient game from Mesopotamia.

1645
A Jesuit missionary composed "The Huron Carol".

The Second Expedition

In August 1671 LaSalle, Nika and six or eight others left Montréal and paddled across Lake Ontario. They portaged at the Niagara River to get to Lake Erie and on to Lake Huron. They travelled up the western side of Lake Huron, through the Straits of Mackinac and into Lake Michigan to Green Bay. From there they travelled south to the Chicago River and via the Des Plaines River to the Illinois River. By then it was the winter of 1672. They turned back when they reached the Mississippi River rather than continuing and risking meeting the Spanish, who controlled the Gulf of Mexico at the mouth of the river. Instead of retracing their route, they travelled on the Kankakee River, portaged to the St. Joseph River [River of the Miami], near present-day South Bend, and from there to Lake Michigan.

LaSalle was the first European to find the Illinois and the Mississippi Rivers. He kept quiet about these discoveries because he did not want other groups travelling into the Illinois and Mississippi Valleys to set up trading posts.

Father Hennepin at Niagara Falls, 1678
by C.W. Jefferys (after Hennepin)

Louis de Buade, Comte de Frontenac

The new Governor of New France, Comte de Frontenac, arrived in September 1672. His family had been closely associated with royalty so he understood the importance of ceremonies and style. In France he had had financial problems and marriage problems. He saw this appointment in New France as a fresh start.

Frontenac was a fine speaker, diplomat and planner. LaSalle spent the winter of 1673 in Québec where he had many conversations with Frontenac. LaSalle's plan to open the Mississippi Valley to trade and transport goods through the Gulf of Mexico to Europe was exciting to him. Not only was there the prospect of making money, but also LaSalle would claim for France all the lands that drained into the Mississippi River and its tributaries. Having that territory would limit the expansion of the English in New England to the east side of the Appalachian Mountains. Together they hatched a plan that would bring France power and new territory and bring them fame, glory and money.

The first step was to build a fort on Lake Ontario at the mouth of the Cataraqui River, [Kingston]. Frontenac needed permission from France to go ahead with his plans, so he kept them secret until November when the last ship left for France. This strategy gave him 18 months to continue before the authorities in France might stop him. He sent Marquette and Jolliet to explore the upper Mississippi River, while LaSalle built Fort Frontenac. This fort would protect the entrance to the St. Lawrence River and be a trading post.

Frontenac planned an elaborate ceremony to impress the Iroquois with the power of France and to honour them. An impressive array of boats and men assembled at Lachine for the trip to Fort Frontenac, with 120 canoes, sacks of food, gifts for the chiefs, 400 Canadians and 50 Huron. Historian John Upton Terrell describes Frontenac's dramatic arrival:

Frontenac and the Iroquois by J.D. Kelly (1862-1958)

As he approached his destination, Frontenac arranged his forces in divisions. In the lead were four squadrons of canoes carrying coureurs de bois chanting and singing, inspired to exuberance by extra rations of liquid spirits. Next came two flatbarges mounting cannon and heavily loaded with equipment and tools. These were followed by large canoes in which rode Frontenac, his guards, and his staff and the gentlemen and ex-officers who had been invited to participate in the journey. Next came the troops, their guns held in plain view, and at the rear were more noisy woodsmen. From every craft flags and pennants whipped in the brisk breeze coming down the river. Plumes waved, and doublets and cloaks and rough woodland garb splashed innumerable colours over the nautical parade.

La Salle had gathered Five Nations chiefs along with their warriors, wives and children to meet Frontenac. They all watched as the Frenchmen pitched tents, stored supplies, built fires and prepared food. This display was planned to show the Five Nations the abilities and power of the French.

The next day the chiefs were invited to sit on sailcloth in front of the Governor's tent. Frontenac appeared in a long scarlet cloak with gold decorations and new leather boots. He sat in a chair looking down on the Iroquois and shared the pipe of peace with them. Chief Garakontie welcomed the Governor to the land of the Iroquois. Although Frontenac addressed the Chiefs as "my children", they liked what he had to say about coming into their midst in peace. Frontenac gave all the chiefs gifts of tobacco and then ended the meeting. At the same time, work began on the fort. Storehouses, homes and palisades took shape as they watched.

After three days of being host to the chiefs, warriors and their families, Frontenac gave a warning. He pointed out the ability of the French to be fine hosts in time of peace, but if angered, they were even more effective in war. The Iroquois were happy with the location of the fort because they could bring their furs to Fort Frontenac, thereby avoiding the long trip down the Hudson River to the British forts.

Although Fort Frontenac was a successful endeavour for Frontenac, La Salle and the Iroquois, it was not welcomed by the merchants in Montréal. They feared financial loss as trading moved west.

In 1675 while in France, LaSalle petitioned for permission to continue his explorations. New France needed to enlarge its territory in order to increase trade. There was also an advantage to moving goods through the Gulf of Mexico to Europe because shipments could be made all year from a warm water port. The King granted LaSalle Fort Frontenac and the islands in the area. He was also given permission to continue to explore. On his way back to New France, he met Father Louis Hennepin who travelled with LaSalle on later expeditions.

LaSalle returned to France in 1677. He needed a ship to sail on the Great Lakes because there were no roads or large navigable rivers. During his visit LaSalle met Henri de Tonty, the son of a banker. Tonty used an iron hand device covered with a glove in place of his hand, which was shot off in a battle. The friends left France with enough money to build a ship.

Buffalo

LaSalle had control legally and permanently of the immense fur trade from south of the Great Lakes and he was given exclusive rights to trade in buffalo skins. His monopoly in the trading business caused anger among the Montréal merchants and the Jesuits who controlled the fur trade from the Great Lakes north and west.

Soon after their return to New France, the supervisor, LaMotte, left Fort Frontenac with carpenters, blacksmiths and their tools and equipment to start building a fort above Niagara Falls. Here they would also build the ship.

1650
The world's population was estimated at 500 million.

1652
The first coffee house opened in London.

1654
The Taj Mahal was completed, commemorating Shah Jahan's favourite wife, Mumtaz Mahal.

The Griffon

In December 1678 La Salle and Tonty left for Niagara Falls aboard a brigantine loaded with shipbuilding supplies, tools, skilled workers and goods to trade with the Native people. At an Iroquois village they employed several young men to hunt in order to provide food for the workers. In exchange, the blacksmith sharpened all the Iroquois hatchets and repaired their rifles in his forge. LaSalle once said, "The blacksmith turned more steel into beaver than the Jesuits turned natives into Christians." The building party continued to the fort above Niagara Falls.

Only the palisade and one house had been built. The local Seneca became unfriendly when they realized that the Europeans were building a fort at the entrance to the upper Great Lakes. The Seneca controlled the fur trade from the interior and did not want to lose their advantageous position to the French. The workers brought from Normandy and Italy did not work well together. All the men were worried that they would be murdered by the Seneca.

The *Griffon* was built and named in honour of Frontenac, whose coat of arms included a winged lion or griffon. In August 1679 LaSalle was able to sail the *Griffon* successfully against the strong current in the Niagara River to reach Lake Erie. With 30 people on board, the *Griffon* reached the Detroit River on August 10. The ship and crew survived a vicious storm on Lake Huron and arrived safely at Fort Michilimackinac.

The Barque "Griffon" (Lake Erie, Ontario), 1679 by Charles H.J. Snider (1879-1971)

1656
Christian Huygens of Holland designed the first pendulum clock.

1656-1680
Kateri Tekawitha, a Mohawk woman, was beatified in 1980.

1657
The first fountain pens were manufactured in Paris.

The people there could not believe their eyes. Some of the men and the Jesuits were not happy to see LaSalle. He had sent some men on ahead to trade, but some of them could not believe that LaSalle would ever arrive, so they were trapping for their own profit. LaSalle knew that he was not popular, but he opened his waterproof case and wearing a crimson cloak with gold braid, a plumed hat and a silver sword, he entered the fort. He had the men, who had disobeyed his commands, arrested and put in irons. LaSalle sent Tonty back to Sault Ste. Marie to track down the men who had deserted.

In early September, LaSalle and his crew set sail for Green Bay on Lake Michigan. This was a happy event because the loyal traders were there with loads of beaver pelts and other valuable furs. Potawatomi Chief Onanghisse greeted LaSalle warmly and presented him with a calumet that would give him safe passage into Native villages on his planned expedition. The *Griffon* was loaded with the furs and sent back to Fort Frontenac.

The LaSalle and the rest of his men continued to the south end of Lake Michigan by canoe. They built Fort Miami while they waited for Tonty to join them. The country was warmer and very beautiful. The Recollet priests collected wild grapes and made communion wine. Members of the Fox tribe warned LaSalle that other traders and the Jesuits were getting the Iroquois to attack the Illinois people living near the Illinois River. LaSalle replied that the French were not

Calumet

This is Father Louis Hennepin's description of the early passport in North America:
It is a large tobacco pipe of red, black, or white marble. The head is finely polished. The quill, which is commonly two and a half feet long (75 cm), is made of pretty strong reed or cane, adorned with feathers of all colours, interlaced with locks of women's hair. Every nation adorns it as they think fit, and according to the birds they have in their country.

Such a pipe is safe conduct amongst all the allies of the nation who has given it; and in all embassies the calumet is carried as a symbol of peace, the savages being generally persuaded that some great misfortune would befall them if they should violate the public faith of the calumet. They fill the pipe with the best tobacco they have and present it to those with whom they have concluded any great affair and smoke out of the same pipe after them.

afraid, so they would continue. However, his men were very fearful. When Tonty arrived with his men, preparations were made for the trek to the Illinois River.

In December 1679 they travelled to the Kankakee portage. This area was a huge swamp that marked the watershed between east-flowing and south-flowing rivers. Eventually, the land became prairie. LaSalle and his men reached a large, deserted village near present-day Utica, Illinois. The Native people were away on their winter hunt. They found corn in the storehouses and took what they needed. Further down the river, they had this encounter recorded by historian John Upton Terrell.

As they floated around the point a village containing eighty to a hundred wigwams came into view. LaSalle again illustrated his thorough understanding of the ways of the Indians. He commanded that the eight canoes be brought abreast. Paddles were stored and the men displayed their guns. Held together, the canoes drifted down the stream, presenting a formidable show of armed might....This Illinois village was thrown into wild confusion. Warriors howled as they took up bows and arrows. Squaws screamed and fled with the children to the trees. Several elderly men advanced to the bank and called out to the strangers to identify themselves. They replied that they were French, (but) still keeping their arms ready and letting the current bear them to a landing place. The Indians, alarmed and intimidated by this bold conduct, immediately presented three calumets.Hennepin recorded that LaSalle "cried out, according to the custom of the tribes, to ask whether they wanted peace or war; it was very important to show courage at the outset.".. A fight was the last thing that LaSalle wanted. Two principal men shortly advanced toward him, holding aloft calumets. Thereupon, LaSalle displayed his own calumet.

The Illinois fear turned to joy and they invited the Frenchmen to their village. LaSalle gave them presents and paid for the corn they had taken from their village. LaSalle said that they had come to tell them about the true God, to trade with them and provide them with arms to help protect themselves. The result was a close alliance between the Illinois and the French.

THE VOYAGE OF THE 'GRIFFON' 1679

First ship to sail Lakes Erie, Huron and Michigan, the "Griffon", probably 40-45 feet long, was built by Robert Cavelier, Sieur de La Salle, several miles above Niagara Falls in 1679. La Salle came to New France in 1667, became seigneur of Cataracoui (Kingston), engaged in the fur trade and sought a western route to China. In August, 1679, the "Griffon" sailed from the Niagara River with La Salle and a company of about thirty-three. In this vicinity the crew had to haul the ship up the swift current of the St. Clair River. La Salle remained in the West while the "Griffon", laden with furs, vanished en route from Green Bay to Niagara.

Archaeological and Historic ... ... of ...

Commemorative Plaque beneath the

Bluewater Bridge in Sarnia, Ontario

Expeditions from 1680-1682

These years were very difficult for LaSalle. While building Fort Crèvecoeur (heartbreak), and a large cargo canoe for transport on the Mississippi River, six men deserted. The local Illinois frightened them with stories of monsters and savage peoples along the river. The hardships of life in the wilderness were new to these men skilled as carpenters and sawyers. After they left, work on the boat was very slow and they needed supplies from the *Griffon* to complete it. LaSalle decided to return to Fort Frontenac and Montréal. He left Tonty at the fort and sent Hennepin and two other men to the mouth of the Wisconsin River.

There was no word of the *Griffon*. While LaSalle was away in Montréal, Tonty went to a safer place called Starved Rock, with three men, to start building a fort. The terrified men left at Fort Crèvecoeur burned the fort and destroyed all but the forge, which Tonty saved. On the boat they had written, "nous sommes tous sauvages" (we are all savages), before they also ran off.

Father Louis Hennepin

Hennepin, Accau and Le Picard were captured by the Sioux and taken north into Minnesota. Sometimes they were badly treated. The following summer they were rescued by Daniel Greysolon du Lhut and four other Frenchmen. They all travelled along the Wisconsin and Fox Rivers to Green Bay. Eventually Hennepin's party went by canoe to Niagara and on to Montréal. In Europe, Hennepin wrote "Description de la Louisiane", published in 1683. In 1697 he published an account of his travels to the Gulf of Mexico, which were all exaggeration and fabrication. This ruined his reputation and he died in disgrace.

In August LaSalle headed west. The Iroquois were on the warpath again because of economic pressures. Fewer beaver, marten, sable, silver fox, and otter pelts were available in their own country due to overtrapping. They couldn't move south because the quality

1658
"The Visible World in Pictures" was the first known children's picture book.

1658
In Sweden, Johann Palmstruck introduced the first bank note.

1658
Delhi became the Mogul capital.

~22~

of the furs was poor. To avoid confrontion, LaSalle travelled up the Humber River [Toronto] to Lake Simcoe and then took the Severn River to Georgian Bay and on to Michilimackinac. He soon left for Fort Miami. The fort was in ruins. He left five men to rebuild it and then departed for the Illinois country.

The large Illinois village had been destroyed and the people massacred by the Iroquois. They found no evidence of Tonty or any other Frenchmen when they searched the remains. Half of the population or 6000 Illinois had been killed.

Hereditary Council of the Iroquois

by Charles Walter Simpson (1878-1942)

LaSalle decided against continuing with such a small band of men, so they went back to Fort Miami. The sight of so many dead must have turned their journey into flight because they covered 320 km (200 mi.) in four days.

La Salle on the Toronto Carrying Place, 1681 by C. W. Jefferys

Although LaSalle had had good relations with the Iroquois in the past, he knew that he had no influence now. He decided to try and build a new alliance of Indian nations to stand against the Iroquois. He held a council to start the process with the Natives who had fled from the East.

1660
The first city coach line opened in Paris.

1662
K'ang-hsi became Emperor of China at age eight.

1664
The British seized New Amsterdam and renamed it New York.

Did you know?

Shipwrecks

There have been hundreds of shipwrecks on the coast of Lake Huron up to Tobermory at the tip of the Bruce Peninsula. A recent excavation on the beach in Southampton unearthed two ships from the 18th century. This plaque, at Tobermory, commemorates the sinking of the *Griffon* in 1679.

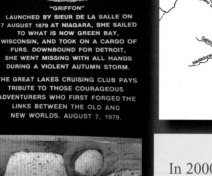

300 YEARS OF UPPER LAKES NAVIGATION

"GRIFFON"

LAUNCHED BY SIEUR DE LA SALLE ON 7 AUGUST 1679 AT NIAGARA, SHE SAILED TO WHAT IS NOW GREEN BAY, WISCONSIN, AND TOOK ON A CARGO OF FURS. DOWNBOUND FOR DETROIT, SHE WENT MISSING WITH ALL HANDS DURING A VIOLENT AUTUMN STORM.

THE GREAT LAKES CRUISING CLUB PAYS TRIBUTE TO THOSE COURAGEOUS ADVENTURERS WHO FIRST FORGED THE LINKS BETWEEN THE OLD AND NEW WORLDS. AUGUST 7, 1979.

La Belle

In 2000, *La Belle* was found in Matagorda Bay with a hold full of the colonists' supplies. The remains of Fort St. Louis, Texas have been found by archaeologists. The artifacts included 8 cannons and a burial site.

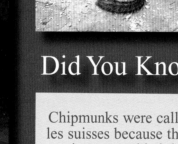

Did You Know?

Chipmunks were called *les suisses* because their stripes resembled the uniforms of the Swiss Guard that protect the pope at the Vatican.

The Welland Canal

The Welland Canal is a busy waterway that connects Lake Ontario to Lake Erie. When LaSalle travelled to Niagara Falls, there was no canal.

Niagara Falls

In October 2003 a man survived a plunge over Niagara Falls with no life-supporting equipment. The authorities charged him with mischief and illegally performing a stunt.

17th Century North America

Did you know?

Madeleine de Roybon d'Allonne

This plaque marks the location near Kingston on Lake Ontario, of the first property in Canada owned by a woman.

Montréal Melon

The Montréal melon was a delicious muskmelon enjoyed in New France in the 17th century. A few farmers are growing it again in the Montréal area.

Places called LaSalle

There are places called LaSalle in Colorado, Illinois, Louisiana, Manitoba, Michigan, Minnesota, Texas, Ontario and Québec, as well as this diner in Montréal.

Fleur-de-lis

Fleur-de-lis refers to the iris. The literal translation is "flower of the lily". This symbol was used on the French Royal Banner, the flag of New France and is the familiar symbol on the Québec flag.

Father Marquette

This moasic is one of four in the lobby rotunda of the Marquette Building in Chicago. The mosaics depict events in Father Marquette's life of exploration south of the Great Lakes.

In March LaSalle and 16 men set out for Illinois country to powwow there. They met hunters from the Fox band who had news that Tonty was living in Green Bay and that Hennepin and his party were safe.

LaSalle met with the Natives and promised that he and his men would support the Illinois and their allies against the Iroquois. The chiefs agreed. Back at the Miami camp, LaSalle met several Iroquois who had been involved in the slaughter at the Illinois village. He confronted them and told them that he despised them and that if they were still there in the morning he would shoot them himself. In the morning they were gone.

When the Illinois tribes were assembled for a ceremony, LaSalle honoured their dead and gave gifts to their memory. He distributed a canoe full of gifts. Then he gave the chiefs six guns for hunting and to defend themselves. Feasts and dancing followed the talks. The western tribes had formed an alliance. An official report to the King stated, "Few men are more adept than LaSalle in the arts of forest rhetoric and diplomacy. He is the greatest orator in North America."

In late May LaSalle and his party left for Michilimackinac where he joined Tonty and Father Membre. Their reunion was joyous. In June they all left for Montréal and Québec.

Later in 1681 LaSalle, along with a large number of cargo canoes, left Fort Frontenac and arrived at the Humber River by mid-September. Father Membre wrote:

M. LaSalle began with his ordinary activity and vast mind, to make preparations for his departure. He selected twenty-three Frenchmen, and eighteen Mohegans and Abnakis, all inured to war. The latter insisted on taking along ten of their women… and three children. This group of 55 people started the huge empire of Louisiana.

In December Tonty left for Illinois country with an advance party of six canoes and 20 men. The rivers were ice-covered, so they built sleds. It was bitterly cold when LaSalle arrived to meet them at the Chicago River in January. For 23 days they dragged their canoes along the icy rivers.

At Lake Peoria there was open water and from then on they floated along the Illinois River to the Mississippi River. In early March the party stopped to hunt at Chickasaw Bluffs. Four hunters went out, but one, Pierre Prudhomme, did not return. They searched for him and on the ninth day he was found wandering in the wilderness, crazy with fear. LaSalle had wanted to reduce the size of the party so that travel could be faster. This was his chance. A fort was built and several Native men, women and children and two Frenchmen stayed to look after Prudhomme.

Discovery of the Mississippi by Marquette, 1673

by J. N. Marchand (1875-1921)

In March the expedition continued. They arrived at a village of Arkansas Natives where Father Membre wrote:

> I cannot tell you the civility and kindness we received from these barbarians, who brought us poles to make huts, supplied us with firewood during the three days we were among them, and took turns feasting us.

Marquette and Jolliet had turned back at this point nine years earlier. No Frenchman had been in this new territory. LaSalle hired two Arkansas guides who took them to the village of a friendly tribe. Their village was large and well established. Membre described the chief's house as:

> 40 feet square, the wall 10 feet high, a foot thick (of mixed mud and straw), and the roof, which was dome shape, about fifteen feet high.

These people had a legend that a grand army in armour and plumes, mounted on horses had passed over the Mississippi River and disappeared into the sky. It was not a legend; it was Hernando DeSoto's army looking for treasure in 1540-1541.

1665
In London the Great Plague killed 68,000 inhabitants.

1665
Cells were discovered by English scientist Robert Hooke.

1666
Isaac Newton measured the moon's orbit.

The travellers lived on wild potatoes and alligator meat supplied by the Native people in their party. On April 6 the river divided into three branches. The group split up and all reached the Gulf of Mexico. On April 9, 1682, LaSalle claimed the land from the Appalachian Mountains to the Rocky Mountains and from the Great Lakes to the Gulf of Mexico for France, and called this vast land, Louisiana. To make sure that the declaration would be legal, LaSalle had brought along a lawyer, Jacques de la Metarie, to sign the document. The next day the expedition turned north.

On the return journey, the Natives they met were not as friendly. There were two outbreaks of fighting and several warriors were killed or wounded. By the time the travellers reached Fort Prudhomme, LaSalle was ill. He may have had a stroke. When he was alert, he gave orders and spoke about his plans for the future.

He sent Tonty to Fort Miami and then

La Salle at the Mouth of the Mississippi, 1682
by J. N. Marchand

on to Québec to tell the news of Louisiana because LaSalle wanted the king to know. Father Membre, Nika and the Native women nursed LaSalle back to health and by August he was able to travel north again. Hundreds of tepees surrounded Fort Miami. LaSalle's plan of an alliance with the various tribes was successful.

When LaSalle arrived in Michilimackinac, Tonty had disturbing news. Governor Frontenac had been recalled to France and the Iroquois were on the warpath and heading west. Changing his plans,

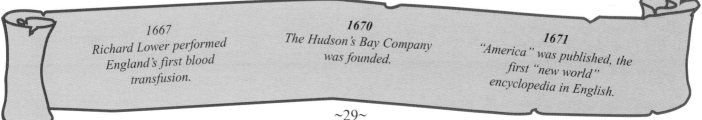

1667
Richard Lower performed England's first blood transfusion.

1670
The Hudson's Bay Company was founded.

1671
"America" was published, the first "new world" encyclopedia in English.

LaSalle decided to go back to Starved Rock with Tonty and his men. They built Fort St. Louis, which was surrounded by lodges, bark huts and log houses occupied by the Illinois and their allies. They grew crops of melons, corn and squash. Native people, 14,000 in all, had moved into Illinois country. LaSalle had built a strong alliance in the West. He had 4,000 warriors, most with rifles. Now he needed the supplies that he had promised them.

LaSalle sent a party to Montréal with furs to trade. He also sent a letter to the new governor, LaBarre, asking that his men be given assistance. No one returned. LaSalle realized that he had to travel to Québec City himself. He arrived in late November but spoke to no one. LaSalle, Nika and Saget boarded the first ship available and sailed for France.

King Louis XIV was still quietly supportive of LaSalle and gave him an audience, which was a rare privilege. LaSalle left the palace with the authority to lead an expedition to the mouth of the Mississippi River and set up a colony.

The Final Expedition

On July 24, 1684, LaSalle left France with four ships and about 400 people consisting of 100 soldiers, workmen, families and their children, orphaned girls looking for husbands, an engineer; Liotot, a physician; eight merchants; LaSalle's brother, Abbé Cavelier; two nephews, Moranget and Cavelier; a friend from his youth called Joutel; Fathers Membre and Zenobe, as well as Saget and Nika. A 36-gun warship, the *Joly*, was sailed by Captain Beaujeu. He was angry that he had to take orders from LaSalle, who had no naval experience. The voyage was difficult and beset by problems. LaSalle kept his plans to himself because they had been sabotaged before. There had been two attempts on his life by poisoning and Governor LaBarre had seized his property at Fort Frontenac. King Louis ordered the restitution of his property but the King could not protect LaSalle from all treachery.

The ships were very crowded and it was hot. One of the supply ships carrying lard, flour, kettles, and ammunition was captured by the Spanish. Instead of following the coast of Florida once they entered the Gulf of Mexico, they crossed diagonally and overshot the Mississippi River by 240 km (150 mi.). At Matagorda Bay [Texas] the passengers and crew set up a temporary fort, but moved to a more favourable spot which LaSalle called Fort St. Louis. When LaSalle came back from exploring, the settlers were thriving. Unfortunately, one ship, *La Belle*, went down in Matagorda Bay because the captain was drunk.

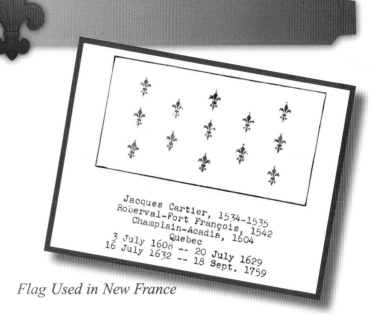

Flag Used in New France

During their three years at Fort St. Louis, LaSalle was seriously ill several times. The years of physical and mental hardship had taken their toll. When he was well, he continued to lead expeditions to find the Mississippi River.

In early 1687 LaSalle set out on another expedition with 16 men, including: Abbé Cavelier, his nephews, Cavelier and Moranget, Joutel, Elder Duhaut, Heins, Liotot, Saget, and Nika. Buffalo and deer were plentiful. Father Cavelier wrote of the friendly Caddo, "Thirty well-mounted young warriors took us by as well beaten a road as that from Paris to Orléans". On March 13 they reached the Brazos River.

Aventures mal heureuses du Sieur de la Salle (from Louis Hennepin)

The horses swam across and the men went by canoes provided by their guides. Joutel described the country as, "A pleasanter country than we had passed through." On March 16, after a buffalo hunt, Moranget was instructed by LaSalle to prepare the meat and then bring it back to the main camp. Moranget had a violent argument with Elder Duhaut, Liotot and Heins. The complaints and dissatisfaction had been building up throughout the journey. These three men attacked Moranget, Nika and Saget while they slept and killed them all. When LaSalle came to find out what was delaying his men, he was ambushed. Elder Duhaut shot him in the temple and he died instantly.

The End of the Expedition

Elder Duhaut took over as leader. The party continued travelling northeast. Fighting continued among the men. Heins shot Duhaut dead and Liotot was wounded so severely that they killed him also. Heins then led the expedition. Father Cavelier suggested continuing to the Mississippi River. The party separated into two groups. Father Cavelier, Joutel and five others got to the Mississippi River. In late July they met coureurs de bois where the Arkansas and Mississippi Rivers meet. They were overjoyed. Together, they decided not to report LaSalle's murder. After spending the winter at Fort St. Louis in Illinois, with Tonty, they travelled back to New France. They sold furs along the way to raise money and when they reached Québec, they sailed for France.

Later, when Tonty was told of LaSalle's death, he took five Frenchmen and three Natives and headed down the Mississippi River to Fort St. Louis in Texas. Caddos he met along the way told him that the settlers had been attacked and killed by a band of Natives from the area. The Native women

1672-1725
Czar Peter the Great famously worked as a labourer in order to better understand the everyday world.

1675
"Britannia", the first national road atlas, was published.

1682
Edmund Halley identified Halley's Comet.

saved four children from death and two young men were taken prisoner. The children were eventually rescued by the Spanish Captain de Leon. Only twelve people are known to have survived that final expedition and returned to France.

In 1869 historian Francis Parkman wrote:

Never under the impenetrable mail of paladin or crusader, beat a heart of more intrepid mettle than within… the breast of LaSalle. To estimate aright the marvels of his patient fortitude one must follow on his tract through the vast scene of interminable journeying, those thousands of weary miles of forest, marsh and river, where again and again, in the bitterness of baffled striving the untiring pilgrim pushed forward towards a goal which he was never to attain.

Joutel wrote the following eulogy about his childhood friend:

LaSalle died at a time when he might have entertained his greatest hopes, as the reward of his labours. He had a capacity and a talent to make his enterprise successful. His constancy and his courage, his indefatigable body would have procured a glorious end to his undertakings had not all those excellent qualities been counterbalanced by too haughty a behaviour, which sometimes made him insupportable, and by a rigidness towards those under his command, which at last drew on him implacable hatred and was the occasion of his death.

LaSalle Leaving Fort St. Louis, Texas

by J. N. Marchand

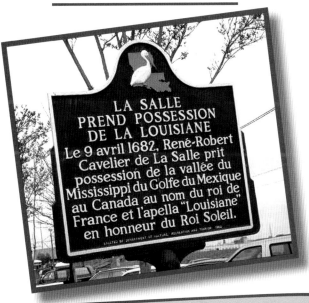

Commemorative Plaque beside the

Mississippi River in New Orleans

1682
Spanish missionaries built the first two missions in Texas.

1683
Anthony van Leeuwenhoek invented the microscope.

1685
All Chinese ports were opened to foreign trade.

IROQUOIS

Name
- Called themselves Haudensaunee (People of the Longhouse)
- Iroquois is the Algonquian word for snake

Location
- South of St. Lawrence River and Lakes Ontario and Erie [Québec, Vermont and New York]

Community
- Clan system headed by clan mother
- Each clan's longhouse named after an animal
- Two people from same clan could not marry because they were related

Customs
- Maple Sap Festival in spring
- Time of Thanksgiving in late autumn - always included prayers of thanksgiving, feasting, dancing and singing
- Midwinter Festival in late January - new babies given clan names, hunters returned from fall hunt

Beliefs
- A creator made all people to care for the earth and all living things
- Everything on the earth had a spirit, some were good and helpful, others evil and brought illness and poor harvests

Interesting Facts
- First Nations Confederacy formed around 1570, was the first democratic organization in North America. Early leaders of the United States were impressed. Thomas Jefferson used ideas from the Confederacy as bases for parts of the U.S. Constitution
- Invented the game of lacrosse, now popular in Canada, U.S. and Europe
- No two living members of the same clan have the same name

MIAMI

Name
- Miami

Location
- Mid 1600's near Green Bay, then moved south to Wabash, Great Miami and Maumee Rivers
- Today about 3000 live in Indiana and 1200 in Oklahoma

Community
- Built dome-shaped wigwams with villages surrounded by cornfields
- Travelled west to hunt buffalo

Interesting Facts
- Had reputation as skilled warriors
- Used elm bark, reeds and butternut because there were no birch trees

Native Peoples

ILLINOIS

Name
- Illini (Superior Men)

Location
- Illinois, southern Wisconsin, Iowa, Missouri

Community
- Several families lived together in bark-covered cabins with arched roofs
- Raised corn, hunted buffalo
- Illinois Confederacy consisted of at least six tribes related to the Miami and controlled Illinois country until 1660, when the Iroquois attacked them

Customs
- Men and women tattooed their bodies
- Men shaved their heads leaving a lock of scalp hair and hair in front of and behind their ears

Interesting Facts
- Prehistoric Natives built burial and temple mounds - over 1000 still stand in Illinois. Monks Mound near Cahokia is the largest in the United States

POTAWATOMI

Name
- Called themselves Neshabe (True People)
- Part of the Algonquian language group
- Closely allied with Chippewa and Ottawa Nations

Location
- North shores of Lakes Superior, Michigan and Huron, then by 1700 moved to Chicago, Detroit and St. Joseph River areas

Community
- Raised corn, squash, pumpkins, made maple sugar, hunted buffalo
- Lived in dome-shaped wigwams covered with bark

Interesting Facts
- Their name for clan was 'dodem', which became totem in English
- Their name for Chicago was Checagou
- They gave a warm welcome to first European, Jean Nicolet

CADDO

Name
- Kadohadacho (Real Chiefs) -later called Tejas (friends)

Location
- Louisiana, Arkansas, Texas, many now live in Oklahoma

Community
- Chiefs highly respected, carried on litters or shoulders of the people
- Built large houses supported by post framework, covered with grass
- Several families lived together
- Houses arranged around large area used for games, rituals, dances, music

Interesting Facts
- Made clothing of skins and fibres
- Made wooden dugout canoes, cane rafts, had horses
- Grew 2 crops per year of corn, beans, squash
- Painted their bodies with bright paints, tattooed with birds, animals, and flowers

Mississippi River

Original Names
- Messipi
  (Ojibwa for big river)
- Meezeeseebee
  (Father of Waters)
- Meschasipi (Chippewa)

Source
- Lake Itasca (Minnesota)

River Mouth
- Delta at the Gulf of Mexico

Length
- 3781 km (2350 mi.)

Industries and Transportation
- Seafood, oil and natural gas in the Gulf of Mexico
- Cotton, peanuts, rice and soybeans
- Tourism

Cities and Towns
- Memphis, Natchez, Baton Rouge, New Orleans, St. Louis

Interesting Facts
- Explored by Hernando De Soto 1540-1541
- People who live nearby just call it 'the river'

Tributaries
- Over 40 tributaries

Missouri

Original Name
- May be named for Native village called Oue Messouri (town of large canoes)

Source
- Three Forks, Montana

River Mouth
- Confluence near St. Louis, Missouri

Length
- 4130 km (2566 mi.)

Industries and Transportation
- Corn, soybeans, wheat, farm products and supplies
- Little activity on the middle and upper river today

Cities and Towns
- Kansas City, Sioux City, Omaha, Great Falls, Leavenworth

Interesting Facts
- Daniel Boone founded and settled at Defiance
- Badlands of S. Dakota are along the White River, a tributary
- First Europeans were Marquette and Jolliet in 1673
- Steamboats began in 1819

Tributaries
- Kansas, Milk, Yellowstone Rivers

A Typical Mississippi Paddlewheeler

The Mississippi River and Its Tributaries

Ohio River

Original Name	• Ohio "something great" (Iroquois)
Source	• Starts at Pittsburgh where the Allegheny and Monongahela Rivers meet
River Mouth	• Confluence at Cairo, Illinois
Length	• 1580 km (982 mi.)
Industries and Transportation	• Coal, agricultural products • Steel, chemicals, rock, gravel moved on barges pushed by tug boats
Cities and Towns	• Pittsburgh, Cincinnati, Louisville
Interesting Facts	• Explored by Daniel Boone and sons in 1799 • LaSalle, first European in 1669
Tributaries	• Wabash, Tennessee, Cumberland, Muskingum, Big Sandy Rivers

Illinois River

Original Name	• French corruption of Illini or Iliniwek Indians
Source	• Starts where Kankakee and Des Plaines Rivers meet near Joliet, Illinois
River Mouth	• Confluence near Alton, Illinois
Length	• 800 km (497 mi.)
Industries	• Coal, peat, corn, soybeans, hogs, cattle, • Farm machinery
Cities and Towns	• Peoria
Interesting Facts	• First Europeans on the river were Marquette and Jolliet in 1673
Tributaries	• Spoon, La Moyne, Mackinaw Rivers and Apple Creek

Arkansas River

Original Name	• Named for the Arkansas Indians (the Quapaw tribe were called "downstream people")
Source	• Rises on the east slope of the Rocky Mountains
River Mouth	• Confluence near Greenville, Mississippi
Length	• 3220 km (2001 mi.)
Industries	• Minerals, natural gas, petroleum • Soybeans, rice, cotton, chickens
Cities and Towns	• Little Rock, Wichita, Tulsa, Fort Smith
Interesting Facts	• Explored by De Soto in 1541 Marquette and Jolliet in 1673 • Royal Gorge walls rise over 300 m (1000 ft.)
Tributaries	• Canadian, Cimarron, White Rivers

Pittsburgh in 2005

Acadia

Acadia was an area of New France that included New Brunswick, Nova Scotia, Gaspé, southern Québec and Prince Edward Island. Right from the beginning there were many difficulties for the settlers. In 1604 Champlain established a fort on the St. Croix River. Because the winter was extremely harsh, 35 of the 79 settlers died of scurvy. The survivors moved to Port Royal, across the Bay of Fundy. This location was more sheltered and for three years they prospered. The French got along well with the Mi'kmaq and Abenaki Nations. Crops were plentiful and in 1607 everyone survived the winter. De Monts, their benefactor, lost exclusive rights to the fur trade. The settlers could not stay because money from the fur trade paid their wages. Most returned to France.

In 1608 Poutrincourt took over Port Royal but he could not finance a supply ship until 1610. Many buildings were in need of repair. Deeds were given to the colonists so that they could own their land. On June 24 Memberton, the Mi'kmaq Chief, and 20 members of his family were baptized. Word of this progress was sent to the king. Even so, no money came to support the colony. Eventually, Madame de Guercheville financed the colony in return for title to all the property except Port Royal.

Being located between New England and New France made Acadia vulnerable.

The first assault from New England was led by Captain Argall in 1613. He attacked French ships and destroyed St. Croix and Port Royal. England and France were not at war, so the settlements were returned to France. Control of Acadia see-sawed back and forth. In 1631 Cardinal Richelieu, in Québec City, wanted to keep Acadia strong as a defence against the English colonies. Forty Scottish settlers at Port Royal were sent back to Scotland because Acadia was under French rule once again.

While the French and English were battling for control of Acadia, the settlers farmed, fished, did lumbering and traded moose, beaver and otter furs. In the Minas Basin, the Comeaus, Landrys, LeBlancs and Thibideaus were inventing and perfecting a system of dikes called 'aboiteaux'. These dikes reclaimed the rich farmland from the sea while preventing the land from being flooded at high tide.

Expatriation of the Acadians

The Acadians tried to remain neutral politically because they depended on trade from both New England and France for their survival. Eventually, under British rule in 1750, they were not allowed to remain neutral. If they did not pledge loyalty to England, they were charged with treason. Those that would not pledge allegiance were deported. The expulsion began in 1755 and continued for eight years. A total of 12,000 Acadians were displaced; the majority went to Louisiana and France. The sea voyages killed 30 percent and more died of diseases when they arrived in their new homes. In 1764 the exile was lifted and many Acadians returned and today flourish in New Brunswick, Nova Scotia, Prince Edward Island and around the world.

Madeleine de Verchères (miniature watercolour on ivory) by Gerald Sinclair Hayward (1845-1926)

Madeleine de Verchères

On October 22, 1692, an Iroquois band surprised the inhabitants of Fort Verchères while they were harvesting the fields. Some people were killed and a few taken prisoner, but 14 year old Madeleine managed to escape by running back to the fort. A warrior chased after her and he had hold of her headscarf, which she surrendered to him just before she slammed the doors shut and bolted them. She immediately put on a soldier's hat and shot the cannon to make the war party believe that there were soldiers at the fort. She took command, told the frightened women to be silent, and ordered her younger brothers to fire their rifles at the attackers. They retreated. The fort was saved.

Her heroism was not acknowledged until several years later when she asked for a pension from the government for her service and was given one. In France, around the same time, Philis de la Tour du Pin de La Charce acted heroically in the Dauphiné region. She gathered citizens together and led them to resist an invasion by the Duke of Savoy. Philis had taken an unusual leadership role for a woman. She was also recognized with a pension.

Madeleine was honoured because her behaviour, though unusual for a woman, showed the loyalty of colonists to the king and their passionate love of New France. Governor General Earl Grey was influential in having a statue of her sculpted by Louis Phillipe Hébert in 1913, which now stands on Verchères bluff overlooking the St. Lawrence River.

Pierre-Esprit Radisson and Médard Chouart des Groseilliers

Radisson came to New France as a youngster during the Iroquois wars. He was captured by the Iroquois in 1651 and adopted into a Native family. He escaped two years later. While he was a captive, Sieur des Groseilliers married Radisson's half-sister. The brothers-in-law were great adventurers. In 1659-60 they canoed to Lake Superior to trade for furs. While there, they saw copper lying on the ground. The Natives told them that the nearby mountain was made of copper. They built a fort on Chequamegon Bay, near present-day Duluth, to set up trade with the Natives.

Radisson and Groseilliers returned to Québec with $300,000.00 worth of furs, enough money to support New France for the year. They had traded without obtaining the proper licence from the government, nor had they co-operated with the Jesuits who wanted to accompany them on their trading expedition. All their furs were confiscated and Groseilliers was imprisoned. This treatment angered them, so at the first opportunity they approached the British about moving the fur trade through Hudson Bay.

These events set the scene for the next chapter in the history of North America: the struggle between Britain and France for control of the continent.

La Salle Monument beside the Lachine Canal

in Montréal

Conclusion

LaSalle's friend, Joutel, said, "By force of will he found solutions to everything which lifted even the most dejected spirits." Historian Douay wrote, "It would be difficult in history to find in a man more intrepid and invincible courage than was shown by Monsieur de LaSalle in adverse circumstances."

As a result of LaSalle's actions, New France expanded to include the huge territory between the Appalachian and Rocky Mountains and from the Great Lakes to the Gulf of Mexico. This expansion was the result of visionaries such as Talon and Frontenac and years of exploration and alliance building by LaSalle. Even though these actions and ambitions were controversial, the expansion of the French Empire was accomplished.

The French, in New France, were primarily concerned with expanding trade in North America; the British, in New England, were primarily concerned with expanding settlement. These two ambitions clashed repeatedly as the fur trade and settlement expanded in North America.

Glossary

Allegiance: the loyalty or obligation of a person to his country

Ambushed: to be attacked unexpectedly

Audience: a formal interview with a person of authority

Calumet: a peace pipe used as a passport for safe passage through Native territory

Confiscated: to take over property by public authority

Confluence: the flowing together of streams or rivers: the place where they join

Controversial: open to argument

Emigrate: to leave one's own country and settle in another

Legitimate: lawful; rightful

Indefatigable: tireless

Insupportable: unbearable

Interminable: endless

Intrepid: fearless, brave

Livre: an old French monetary unit, worth one pound of silver

Manitou: something having supernatural powers; the power or spirit that rules nature

Mission: the establishment of a religious settlement to convert people to the religion of the missionaries

Paladin: the champion of a cause

Reformation: a religious movement begun by Martin Luther in the 16th century that resulted in the establishment of several Protestant churches

Remnant: a small piece or part that is left over

Surrender: to give up under pressure to the authority of another; yield

Temple: a building dedicated to the worship of God

More to Do ... Novels for Young People

Carter, Anne. THE GIRL ON EVANGELINE BEACH. Toronto: Stoddart Kids, 2000. Readers aged 12 and up will enjoy this time travel adventure set just before the expulsion of the Acadians.

Charles, Veronika Martenova. MAIDEN OF THE MIST : A LEGEND OF NIAGARA FALLS. Toronto: Stoddart Kids, 2001. The myth of Lelawala, a timeless heroine of the Falls, is beautifully retold.

Emery, Joanna. BROTHERS OF THE FALLS. New York: Silver Moon Press, 2004. In 1847, orphaned Irish brothers face tragedy and separation on their way to a new life near Niagara Falls.

Martel, Suzanne. THE KING'S DAUGHTER. Toronto: Groundwood, 1980 and 1994. When 18 year old Jeanne has an opportunity to sail to New France in 1672 to marry a stranger, she leaps at the chance.

McKay, Sharon E. ESTHER. Toronto: Penguin Canada, 2004. This is a fictionalized account of the 1738 story of the Jewish girl who arrived in New France disguised as a Catholic boy. For students in grade 7 and up.

Metikosh, Anne. TERRA INCOGNITA. Vancouver: Ronsdale Press, 2000. In 1670, Madeleine disguises herself as a boy to make the canoe trip from Montréal to Michilimackinac in search of her father.

North, Sterling. CAPTURED BY THE MOHAWKS AND OTHER ADVENTURES OF RADISSON. Boston: Houghton Mifflin, 1960. After his teenage years of capture and adventure, Radisson visited the courts of Europe and founded the Hudson's Bay Company.

Rawlyk, George and Mary Alice Downie. A SONG FOR ACADIA. Halifax: Nimbus, 2004. Originally entitled "A Proper Acadian", this is the tale of an Acadian boy of both English and French parentage who is caught in the deportations of 1755.

Stewart, Sharon. BANISHED FROM OUR HOME :THE ACADIAN DIARY OF ANGÉLIQUE RICHARD. Markham, ON: Scholastic, 2004. Families are virtually torn apart during the days of the expulsion of the Acadians.

Taylor, C.J. PEACE WALKER: THE LEGEND OF HIAWATHA AND TEKANAWITA. Toronto: Tundra, 2004. The author has drawn on her Mohawk heritage to tell the story of how courageous Chief Hiawatha brought the Great Peace to the Iroquois Confederacy.

Trottier, Maxine. ALONE IN AN UNTAMED LAND: THE FILLES DU ROI DIARY OF HÉLÈNE ST. ONGE. Markham, ON: Scholastic, 2003. Frightened and on her own, Hélène struggles for survival in New France.

Trottier, Maxine. SISTER TO THE WOLF. Toronto: Kids' Can Press, 2004. In 1703, Cécile speaks out against the mistreatment of Native slaves in New France. For readers 10 to 14.

Walsh, Ann (editor). BEGINNINGS: STORIES OF CANADA'S PAST. Vancouver: Ronsdale Press, 2001. This anthology includes three short stories relating to the years of the rise of New France.

More to Do ... Non-fiction for Young People

Binns, Tristan. LOUIS JOLLIET. Chicago: Heinemann Library, 2001.

Coulter, Tony. LASALLE AND THE EXPLORERS OF THE MISSISSIPPI. New York City: Chelsea House, 2003.

Granfield, Linda. ALL ABOUT NIAGARA FALLS. Toronto: Kids Can, 1988.

Jacobs, William Jay. LASALLE: A LIFE OF BOUNDLESS ADVENTURE. New York City: Franklin Watts, 1994.

Kalman, Bobbie and Niki Walker. LIFE IN AN ANISHNABE CAMP. St. Catharines ON: Crabtree, 2003.

Kalman, Bobbie and Kathryn Smithyman. NATIONS OF THE WESTERN GREAT LAKES. St. Catharines ON: Crabtree, 2003.

Larkin, Tanya. JACQUES MARQUETTE AND LOUIS JOLLIET: EXPLORERS OF THE MISSISSIPPI. New York City: Rosen, 2004.

Livesey, Robert and A.G. Smith. NEW FRANCE. Toronto: Stoddart, 1990.

Moore, Christopher. MATHURIN BROCHU OF NEW FRANCE. Toronto: Grolier, 1988.

Neering, Rosemary. LIFE IN ACADIA. Toronto: Fitzhenry & Whiteside, 2003.

Neering, Rosemary. LIFE IN NEW FRANCE. Toronto: Fitzhenry & Whiteside, 2003.

Nolan, Jeannette Covert. LASALLE AND THE GRAND ENTERPRISE. Lakeville, Connecticut : Grey Castle Press, 1991.

Payment, Simone. LASALLE: CLAIMING THE MISSISSIPPI RIVER FOR FRANCE. New York City : Rosen, 2004.

Quinlan, Don. EXPLORERS AND PATHFINDERS. Markham ON: Fitzhenry & Whiteside, 2004.

Santella, Andrew. SIEUR DE LASALLE. Chicago: Heinemann Library, 2002.

Sonneborn, Liz. THE IROQUOIS. New York City: Franklin Watts, 2002.

Syme, Ronald. BAY OF THE NORTH : THE STORY OF PIERRE RADISSON. New York City: Morrow, 1950.

Websites

Ancient Architects of the Mississippi
www.cr.nps.gov/aad/feature/feature.htm
Sponsored by the U.S. National Park Service, this site offers information about ancient cultures along the Mississippi Valley.

The Canadian Museum of Civilization's Virtual Museum of New France
www.civilization.ca/vmnf
Text, maps and illustrations bring alive the stories of LaSalle and the other great explorers of Canada.

Indian and Northern Affairs Canada
www.ainc-inac.gc.ca
Especially in the Arts, Culture and History section, this site provides information on many aspects of aboriginal history and life, including June 21, National Aboriginal Day.

Pathfinders and Passageways
www.collectionscanada.ca/explorers
Read about the individuals who helped to open up Canada throughout the centuries.

Statistics Canada
www.statcan.ca/english/edu
Students and teachers will find census data from 1665, maps, projects and role-playing ideas, among many other interesting features.

Tracing the History of New France
www.collectionscanada.ca/05/0517/051701-e.html
A wealth of pictures, documents and a game or two await students and adults at this site.

CANADA

NEW BRUNSWICK

Village Historique Acadien, Caraquet
1-877-721-2200
www.villagehistoriqueacadien.com
Costumed interpreters bring ancestral customs and traditional
trades to life covering the years 1770-1793.

NOVA SCOTIA

Fortress of Louisbourg National Historic Site
Cape Breton Island, 902-733-2280
www.parkscanada.pch.gc.ca
Another symbol of the see-saw battle for control of eastern North
America, Louisbourg is the largest reconstructed French fortified
town in North America.

Grand-Pré National Historic Site
Grand-Pré, 902-542-3631
www.parkscanada.pch.gc.ca
Visit this now beautiful spot , the memorial church, exhibits and
monument to understand the Deportation of the Acadians.

ONTARIO

Bruce County Museum
Southampton, 866-318-8889
www.brucecounty.on.ca/museum
Boat Trips! Storms! Shipwrecks!
Mysteries! There is much to do and learn around Lake Huron.

Discovery House Museum
Sarnia, 519-332-1556.
www.timewellspent.ca
Local history and natural history exhibits, as well as possible
relics from the *Griffon,* make this small museum worthy of a visit.

Marine Museum of the Great Lakes
Kingston, 613-542-2261
www.marmuseum.ca
Learn about exploration and shipping methods from ancient
Native civilizations to the present.

Oasis of Peace
Sault Ste. Marie overlooking the St. Mary River Rapids
In 1671, a representative of King Louis XIV and 17 Native
nations sealed a peace agreement with a huge cross.
This was re-erected 300 years later.

Ska-Nah-Doht Iroquoian Village and Museum
Longwoods Road Conservation Area
Mt. Brydges, 519-264-2420
www.lowerthames-conservation.on.ca
Enjoy a re-created Iroquoian village of 1000 years ago with
hands-on exhibits, nature trails and a boardwalk.

QUÉBEC

Château Ramezay
Montréal, 514-861-3708
www.chateauramezay.qc.ca
Many special events and changing exhibits portray the colourful
history of Canada, especially Montréal.

Lachine Canal National Historic Site
Montréal, 514-283-6054
www.parkscanada.pch.gc.ca
Now re-opened as a pleasure boat waterway, the Canal and its
environs have been renovated and restored.

Maison Saint-Gabriel
Montréal, 514-935-8136
www.maisonsaint-gabriel.qc.ca
Exhibitions, gardens, re-enactments,
the story of the King's Daughters
and Marguerite Bourgeoys can
be enjoyed here.

McCord Museum
Montréal, 514-398-7100
www.mccord-museum.qc.ca
Embark on a voyage through Canada's history in the heart of
downtown Montréal.

Tsiionhiakwatha Droulers Site
Saint-Anicet, 450-264-3030
www.sitedroulers .ca
Travel to the 15th century and immerse yourself in the daily life of
pre-contact Iroquois people.

THE UNITED STATES

ARKANSAS

Arkansas Post National Memorial
Gillett, 870-548-2207
www.nps.gov/arpo
Tonty, Jolliet, Marquette and LaSalle all reached this site which is
now on the Arkansas River because the Mississippi has changed
its course.

ILLINOIS

Starved Rock State Park
near LaSalle, 815-667-4906
www.dnr.state.il.us
Fort St. Louis, built here by LaSalle in 1682, functioned until
1702. A group of Illinois people took refuge here in 1769 but
died of starvation.

Places to Visit

IOWA

National Mississippi River Museumand Aquarium
Dubuque, 800-226-3369
www.mississippirivermuseum.com
At this affiliate of the Smithsonian, enjoy dynamic aquariums, historical exhibits, a stroll through the wetlands and a boatyard.

LOUISIANA

Acadian Cultural Center
Jean Lafitte National Historical Park and Preserve
Lafayette, 337-232-0789
www.nps.gov/jela
"Acadian" became "Cajun"and this centre offers exhibits on all aspects of Cajun life and culture.

Acadian Memorial,
St. Martinville, 337-394-2258
www.acadianmemorial.org
The story of the Acadian exile is re-told in a mural, plaques and a multi-media history centre to honour the 3,000 people who found refuge in Louisiana.

MICHIGAN

Colonial Michilimackinac
Mackinaw City, 231-436-4100
www.mackinacparks.com/parks
The reconstruction of the Fort (built in 1715) offers costumed re-enactments, exhibits such as a Native encampment and live demonstrations.

Great Lakes Shipwreck Museum
Whitefish Point, 888-492-3747
www.shipwreckmuseum.org
Find out why Michigan has so many lighthouses! Experience the wonders of Lake Superior and stay overnight at the light station..

Museum of Ojibwa Culture and Marquette Mission Park
St. Ignace, 906-643-9161
www.stignace.com
This park is the presumed site of Marquette's grave and the museum has extensive exhibits on Ojibwa history and culture.

River of History Museum
Sault Ste. Marie, 906-632-1999
www.history.eup.k12.mi.us/local/river
From the Anishnabeg Natives to Brûlé to Marquette and later, the history of the St. Mary's River unfolds here.

NEW YORK

Iroquois Indian Museum
Howes Cave, 518-296-8949
www.iroquoismuseum.org
Part of the larger museum, the Children's Museum introduces Iroquois traditions through crafts, games and technologies.

Old Fort Niagara
Youngstown, 716-745-7611
www.oldfortniagara.org
Situated at the mouth of the Niagara River, this beautiful fort depicts life in the late 17th century.

TENNESSEE

Mississippi River Museum
Mud Island River Park
Memphis, 800-507-6507
www.mudisland.com
This amazing museum offers more than 10,000 years of river history through life-size reconstructions.

TEXAS

Corpus Christie Museum of Science and History
Corpus Christie, 361-826-4650.
www.cctexas.com
Visitors can explore many shipwreck stories including *La Belle* and see life-size replicas of Columbus's ships the *Pinta* and the *Santa Maria*.

Matagorda County Museum
Bay City, 979-245-7502
www.matagordacountymuseum.org
A replica of *La Belle* and many of its artifacts are featured here, near the location of LaSalle's final venture.

WASHINGTON, D.C.

National Museum of the American Indian
202-633-1000
www.americanindian.si.edu
With a collection of over 800,000 objects, this innovative museum celebrates indigenous cultures and voices from across the Americas.

WISCONSIN

Chequamegon-Nicolet National Forest
This fabulous forest comprises 1.5 million acres in 4 separate regions. The Great Divide Scenic Byway is named for the ridges which separate waters flowing to Lake Superior and the Mississippi River.

Bibliography

Coates, Colin M. "Warrior Woman: The Legend of Madeleine de Verchères." The Beaver, April/May 2002.

Dennis, Jerry. THE LIVING GREAT LAKES: SEARCHING FOR THE HEART OF THE INLAND SEAS. Boston: St. Martin's Press, 2003.

Eccles, W.J. THE FRENCH IN NORTH AMERICA, 1500-1783. Markham ON: Fitzhenry & Whiteside, 1998.

Eccles, W.J. FRONTENAC: THE COURTIER GOVERNOR. Toronto: McClelland & Stewart, 1968.

Gedeon, Julie. "History's Floodgate: The Lachine Canal Reopens." The Beaver, August/September 2002.

Greer, Allan (editor). THE JESUIT RELATIONS: NATIVES AND MISSIONARIES IN 17TH CENTURY NORTH AMERICA. Boston: Bedford, St. Martin's, 2000.

Lânctot, Gustave. A HISTORY OF CANADA FROM ITS ORIGINS TO THE ROYAL REGIME, 1663. Toronto: Clarke, Irwin, 1963.

Lânctot, Gustave. A HISTORY OF CANADA: VOLUME TWO FROM THE ROYAL REGIME TO THE TREATY OF UTRECHT, 1663-1713. Toronto: Clarke, Irwin, 1964.

Langlois, Nicole (editor). CANADIAN GLOBAL ALMANAC 2004. Toronto: John Wiley and Sons, 2004.

Leduc, Adrienne. "Dear Sieur de LaSalle." The Beaver, April/May 1999.

McLean, Harrison John. THE FATE OF THE GRIFFON. Toronto: Griffin Press, 1974.

McMillan, Alan D. and Eldon Yellowhorn. FIRST PEOPLES IN CANADA. Vancouver: Douglas & McIntyre, 2004.

Muhlstein, Anka. LASALLE: EXPLORER OF THE NORTH AMERICAN FRONTIER. New York City: Arcade, 1994

Parkman, Francis. LASALLE AND THE DISCOVERY OF THE GREAT WEST. New York City: Modern Library, 1999.

Rogers, S. John and Donald Harris. BOLD VENTURES. Toronto: Clarke, Irwin, 1962.

Spurr, Daniel. RIVER OF FORGOTTEN DAYS: A JOURNEY DOWN THE MISSISSIPPI IN SEARCH OF LASALLE. New York City: Henry Holt, 1998.

Terrell, John Upton. LASALLE: THE LIFE AND TIMES OF AN EXPLORER. Toronto: Clarke, Irwin, 1968.

Trudel, Marcel. THE BEGINNINGS OF NEW FRANCE,1524-1663. Toronto: McClelland & Stewart, 1973.

Warkentin, Germaine. CANADIAN EXPLORATION LITERATURE. Don Mills ON : Oxford University Press, 1993.

Weddle, Robert S. WILDERNESS MANHUNT: THE SPANISH SEARCH FOR LASALLE. Austin: University of Texas Press, 1973.

Picture Credits

Abbreviations: BAS Betty Sherwood ; BS Bob Shimer ; CP © Canada Post Corporation (reproduced with permission); LAC Library and Archives Canada; MSWD Main Street Web Design; MD Marilyn Dodds; RC courtesy of Rogers Communication; TPL Toronto Public Library

Cover La Salle Statue MD; page 4 LAC (C-007885); 5 TPL (JRR 4161), CP (1985); 6 CP (1973); 8 RC; 9 CP (1966); 11 MSWD; 13 BAS; 15 LAC (C-069761); 16 LAC (C-070245); 17 RC; 18 TPL; 19 TPL (JRR 1162); 20 TPL; 21 MSWD; 23 LAC (C-073678), (C-013949); 24 MD, BAS, MSWD (3); 26 MSWD (2), BAS, BS; 28 LAC (C-008486); 29 LAC (C-017560); 31 LAC (C-099234), (C-025763); 33 MSWD, LAC (C-004569); 34 TPL; 36 MSWD; 37 MSWD; 38 LAC (C-024563); 39 LAC (C-083513); 40 MSWD; 44 CP (1975); 45 MSWD.

Index

Index